More Fun Than a Barrel o

Wild about Dinosaurs!

by Mike Crowder

For Gwen
The Sweetest Little Thing Ever

Special thanks to Karen Austin
of Tinker & Swag

All contents Copyright 2025, Michael Allan Crowder
GraySheep Graphics

All rights reserved. No portion of this book may be reproduced,
stored in a retrieval system, or transmitted in any form or by any means: electronic,
mechanical, photocopy, recording, claymation, or other -
except for critical reviews or articles, without the prior permission of the publisher.

Published in Ponte Vedra Beach, FLA
L

This Book Belongs to:

_____

About this book

So. **Dinosaurs** ("Terrible Lizards"). Just what do we know about them?

They roamed the Earth for, like, millions of years, then all died off! What...!?! No fair! Can you imagine how cool it would be to see a **brachiosaurus** or **velociraptor**? Or maybe a **quetzlcoatlus**?

What about a **tyrannosaurus rex**, the most *famous* dinosaur ever! The **lion** may be the "king of the beasts," but the **T-Rex** was king of the *dinosaurs*!

Luckily, you have me! I'm here to show you some of the more interesting dinosaurs. I'll tell you what their names mean, how big they were, where they lived, when they lived, and what they ate.

I made some pretty, and *quirky,* pictures!

I even made a few dad jokes!

So, why not take off your shoes, and "set a spell" whilst I tell you about these fascinating **reptiles**.

Also, with few exceptions, there were no dinosaurs that swam or flew, but where's the fun in that? So, I've thrown in some **prehistoric reptiles** you may have *thought* were dinosaurs, as a bonus.

A brief note about the sources: Scouring the internet shows little to no agreement between websites. Each relies on different facts. Some use mistranslations, others use mispronunciations.

And do *not* get me *started* on the pictures!

Speaking of the pictures, *another* brief note about the colors of the dinosaurs: *no-one* knows what colors they were! For all we know, they were paisley, checkered, or even *plaid*! With this in mind, I made my dinosaurs pretty colors. (No plaid!)

Just enjoy!

A is for Allosaurus
(AL-low-SORE-us)

Aa

A is for **Allosaurus** (AL-low-SORE-us),

Archaeopteryx (ARR-key-OP-ter-icks),

Abelisaurus (AY-bel-luh-SORE-us),

and **Apatosaurus** (uh–pat-uh-SORE-us), too!

The **allosaurus** ("different lizard") lived about 150-**million** years ago, in the **Jurassic period**. It was the **apex predator** of its time (an apex predator has no **natural predators**). The allosaurus was not as large as some other **theropods** (the name means, "wild beast feet"). It was 30-feet long, and weighed up to three **tons**.

The allosaurus is believed to be the fiercest dinosaur to *ever* live in **North America**. It was scarier than even the **tyrannosaurus rex**, the apex predator of *its* time.

Theropods were **carnivores** (meat eaters). They were **bipedal**, which means they walked on their **hind** legs. They had three fingers on each "hand," and three toes on each foot. Just like birds, they had hollow bones. Some even had feathers!

Did you know that before T-Rex and **velociraptor** ("swift thief") became the biggest movie stars, the allosaurus starred in "The Lost World"? Made in 1925, it was the first full-length dinosaur movie.

If I were that allosaurus, I would fire my agent!

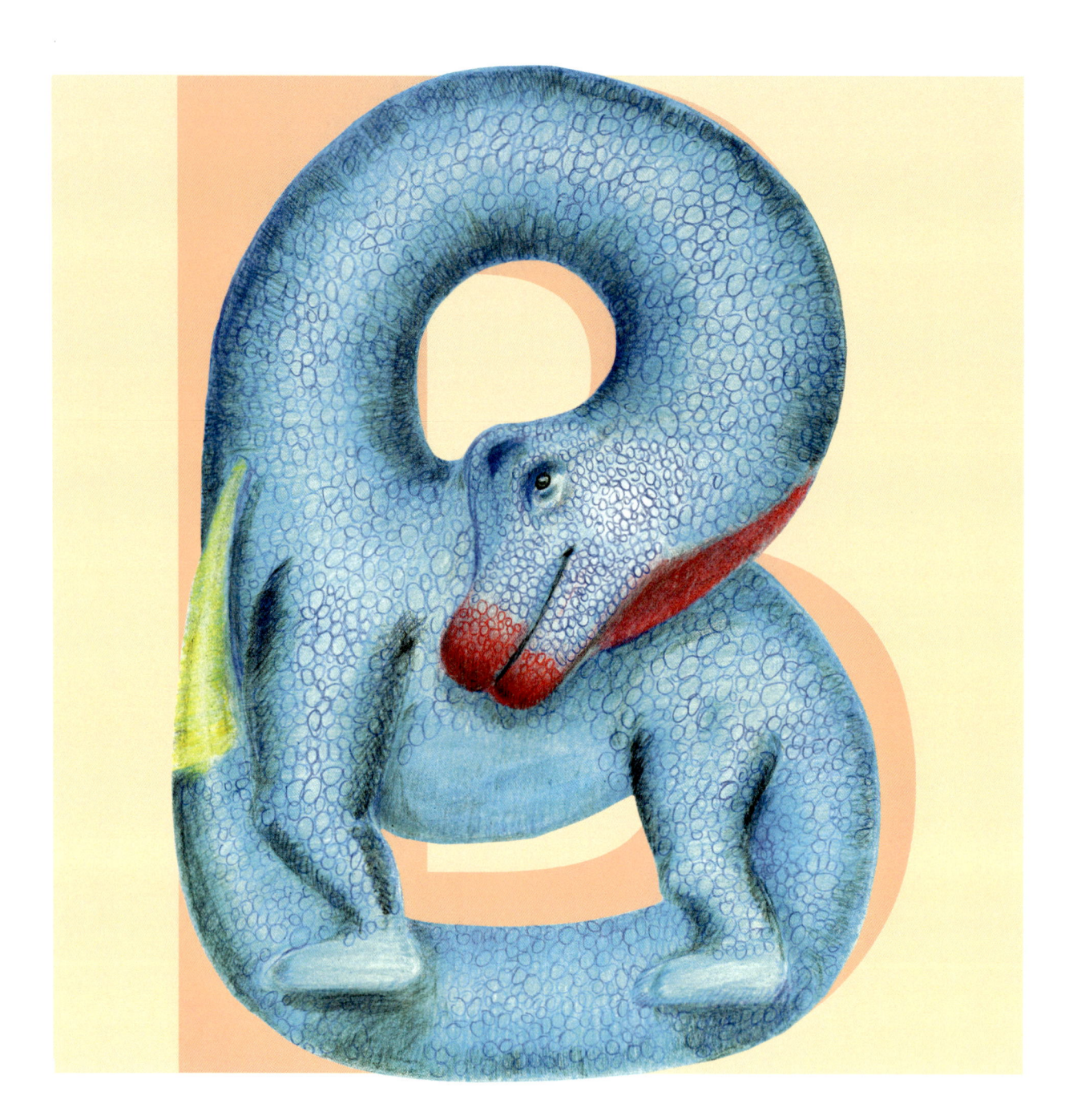

B is for Brachiosaurus

(BRACK-ee-oh-SORE-us)

Bb

Because its front legs were longer than its hind legs, this dinosaur was named **brachiosaurus** ("arm lizard"). It was 85-feet long, from head-to-tail, and weighed up to 50 tons. It lived about 150-million years ago, during the Late Jurassic period. There was a time, before scientists found the **argentinosaurus** ("**Argentinian** lizard"), when the brachiosaurus was believed to be the largest land animal, ever.

It was first discovered by scientists in Colorado. Like all **sauropods** (lizard-foot), the brachiosaurus was a **quadruped** (that means it walked on all four feet), and an **herbivore** (plant-eater). Apparently, being a vegan worked, because scientists think it may have lived to be *100*-years old!

Now friends, had it only lived a few million years *longer*, it *might* have outlived that last argentinosaurus!

C is for Compsognathus
(COMP-sug-NAY-thuss)

Cc

C is for **Compsognathus** (COMP-sug-NAY-thuss),

Chilesaurus (CHEE-lay-SORE-us),

and **Cetiosaurus** (SET-tee-oh-SORE-us), too!

    Compsognathus means "pretty jaw." (Pretty? You call *that* "pretty"?) It was once believed to be the smallest dinosaur, but we now know differently (keep reading). Even though the compsognathus was a very small theropod, it was *still* the largest **fossil** dinosaur to be found in the area when first uncovered in **Germany** in the 1800s. It lived about 150-million years ago, during the Late Jurassic period.

    The compsognathus was only two-feet long, and weighed about five pounds. It ate animals smaller than itself; one fossil was found with the skeleton of a *lizard* in its tummy!

    Eww!

    Because of its size, you might think it had feathers, but unlike *so many* other small theropods, it did not.

    Go figure.

D is for Dimetrodon
(dye-MET-ro-don)

Dd

While it's not known exactly what it ate, the **dimetrodon** ("two measures of teeth") was a carnivore. The most dimetrodon fossils have been found in the southwestern United States.where it lived between 295- and 272-million years ago, during the **Early Permian** period.

The biggest dimetrodon ever found was 15-feet long and weighed 500 pounds! That fancy "sail" on its back was there to control its body temperature.

The dimetrodon *looks* like a dinosaur, and is often mistaken for one. However, it was *really* a type of prehistoric reptile known as a **pelycosaur** ("bowl lizard").

"Bowl lizard"?

…These names can't all be winners!

Hey! It may not be a *real* dinosaur, but it sure makes a great letter "D," doesn't it?!

E is for Elmisaurus
(ELL-mih-SORE-us)

Ee

E is for **Elmisaurus** (ELL-mih-SORE-us),

Eoraptor (EE-oh-rap-ter),

and **Europelta** (YOU-ro-pel-tuh), too!

This is the elmisaurus ("foot sole lizard").
Okay. This is where all the dinosaur stuff gets a *little* tricky. First, depending on to whom you speak, elmisaurus *could* be pronounced, "ELL-*me*-SORE-us" Second, it *could* mean "foot lizard."

The reason it's called "foot sole lizard" is because its feet were different than those of other dinosaurs.

The feet are also the only fossils they have for this dinosaur.

The elmisaurus lived in **Mongolia** 70-million years ago, during the Late **Cretaceous** period. Discovered in 1981, the fossil was only two bones. More bones were uncovered later, but they were just *more* foot bones! No spine, no ribs, no tail, no *skull*. Scientists are not even sure if it had a beak. Or feathers. Just feet... They know it walked on two feet.

Based on other theropods of its type, scientists were able to guess what it *probably* looked like!

They *think*.

F is for Fulgurotherium
(FOOL-grr-oh-THEE-ree-um)

Ff

Like the elmisaurus, the **fulgurotherium** ("lightning beast") is another dinosaur of *unknown* looks. The model was based on only parts of a *thigh bone*! Some teeth and bones belonging to the fulgurotherium have since been found, but no skull. The fulgurotherium was first uncovered on the **Lightning Ridge** in southern **Australia.** It lived in either the early Cretaceous or late Cretaceous period, about 146-million to 55-million years ago. It was what is known as an **ornithopod** ("birdfoot"). As an ornithopod, the fulgurotherium was bipedal. An herbivore, the fulgurotherium is one of the few *non-* **mammals** to be called "therium" (beast).

On the *plus* side, it looks *really* pretty in pink, and has a *really* cool name!

G is for Gojirasaurus
(go-JEE-ruh-SORE-Us)

Gg

G is for **Gojirasaurus** (go-JEE-ruh-SORE-Us),

and **Gigantoraptor** (jye-GAN-to-rap-ter), too!

"Gojira" is what **Japanese** people call the movie-monster "**Godzilla**." **Gojirasaurus** lived, *not* in **Japan,** like you'd think, but in **New Mexico**. It lived in the **Triassic** period between 237- and 201-million years ago. Discovered in 1981, it didn't receive its name until 1997, when Paleontologist Kenneth Carpenter, apparently a big fan of Godzilla, named it "gojirasaurus."

Sure, the tyrannosaurus rex was 40-feet long, and weighed up to nine tons, but at 18- to 20-feet in length and weighing around 800-1,000 pounds, the gojirasaurus was among the largest theropods of its time.

Because scientists think the **fossil remains** may be those of a *young* gojirasaurus; an adult gojirasaurus would have been bigger.

As it was *nowhere* near the size of Godzilla in the movies, it really was *not* much of a threat to large buildings, and forget about those "spitting high-tension wires...!" (ask your grandfather)

H is for Heterodontosaurus
(HEH-der-oh-DON-tuh-SORE-us)

Hh

The **heterodontosaurus** ("different-toothed lizard") from **South Africa**, possibly **Mexico** and **Argentina**, was a small dinosaur called a "**euornithopod**" ("flying foot"). It lived during the Early Jurassic period, 200- to 190-million years ago.

This bipedal heterodontosaurus had a large brain for a dinosaur. Surprisingly large... for a *dinosaur*...!

Did it do math? Could it even count?

Probably not.

It was about 3-feet long, and weighed about 22 pounds. It had small, flat, teeth set back in its jaws, which it used for grinding plants, and big, pointed teeth at the front. These teeth might have been used for protection, *but* could have used for tearing flesh, like a carnivore's. In fact, this dinosaur may have actually been **omnivorous** ("everything eating").

Did you know bears, raccoons, and even *you* are omnivorous? You could eat any *food* you like. Even liver, if you wanted.

(Liver? No thank you!)

I is for Ichthyosaurus
(ICK-thee-oh-SORE-us)

Ii

I is for **Ichthyosaurus** (ICK-thee-oh-SORE-us), and **Isisaurus** (ICE-ih-SORE-us), too!

Like the dimetrodon, the **ichthyosaurus** ("lizard fish") is another prehistoric reptile. It was what they call a **marine, or aquatic, reptile**. The dimetrodon, other reptiles, and the dinosaurs we have looked at so far, all gave birth by laying eggs, but scientists are pretty sure the ichthyosaurus gave birth to live babies! Just like **whales**!

Did you know whale babies (**calves**) are born tail-first, so they don't drown?

Ichthyosaurus was between 6-and-a-half-feet, and 10-feet long. It was the smallest member of a family of carnivores that included the 82-foot long **ichthyotitan** ("giant lizard-fish").

It lived between 201- and 175-million years ago, during the Early Jurassic period, where it ate fish and squid.

J is for Jainosaurus
(JAY-noh-SORE-Us)

Jj

A **titanosaur** ("giant lizard"), the **jainosaurus** ("Jain's lizard") was first discovered in 1871. It was first thought to be an **antarctasaurus** ("southern lizard").

It was not.

In 1995, it was finally named after the **paleontologist** Sohan Lal Jain. The 59-foot long, 33-thousand pound jainosaurus was an herbivore, and a resident of **India**. It lived about 68-million years ago, in the Early Cretacious period. It lived near *another* titanosaur, **isisaurus**.

Now, do you think the two titanosaurs were friends?

If they *were* friends, were they, like, *real* friends? Or do you think maybe they just kind of grunted and nodded when they passed each other in the jungle?

At this point, we still don't know.

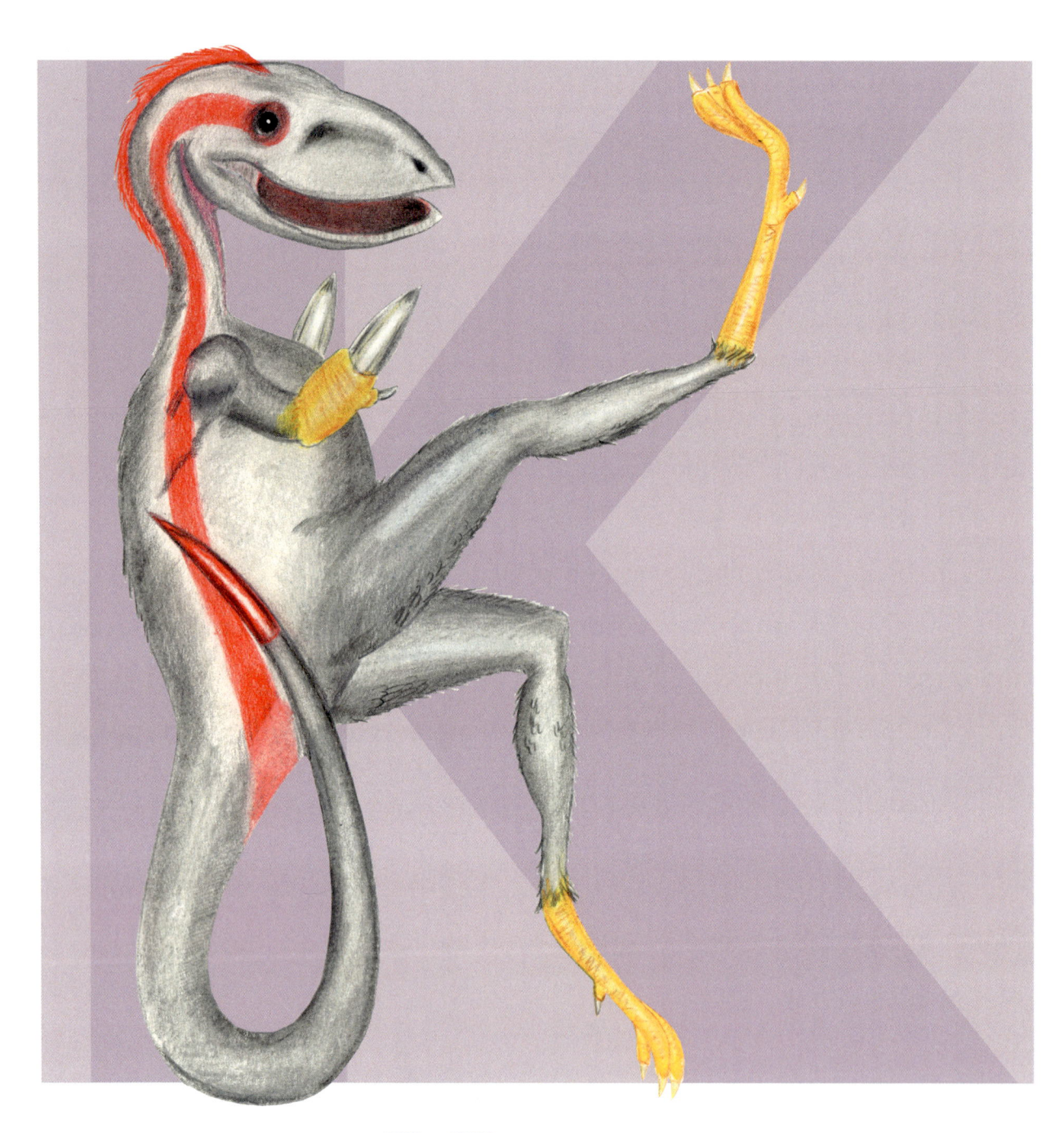

K is for
Kol

(Coal)

Kk

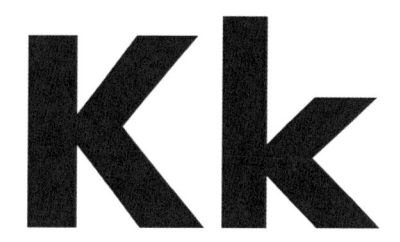

A resident of the **Central-Asian** deserts of **modern Mongolia**, the **kol** (Mongolian for "foot") was about 6-feet long and weighed between 40 and 50 pounds. As you can probably guess, one foot is all that exists of this dinosaur.

(...Just *one* foot!)

Because of that foot, scientists think it is closely related to the **alvarezsaurus** (AL-va-rez-SORE-us), a small, carnivorous, feathered dinosaur from South America.

The kol might have been feathered.

It lived about 75-million years ago, during the Late Cretaceous period.

(...One foot!)

L is for Labocania
(lab-oh-KAY-nee-ah)

Ll

The **labocania** was a type of tyrannosaur that lived in **Mexico**! It lived in the Late Cretaceous period, between 73- and 66-million years ago.

Most of the different tyrannosaurs have been found in more northern areas like **Montana**, and **Canada**. Even the tyrannosaurus rex has been found only as far south as **Wyoming.**

The labocania fossils were found in 2000, then put away in a drawer in Mexico's **Museo del Desierto** in **Saltillo**.

The labocania, like all tyrannosaurs, was a carnivore, and unlike other theropods, had only two fingers on each "hand."

The "fun-sized" tyrannosaur, labocania weighed about 3,000 pounds, and was about 23-feet long.

M is for Microraptor
(MY-crow-rap-ter)

Mm

Smaller than even the compsognathus, the **microraptor** ("tiny thief") weighed only two or three pounds! That's like *three* of your dad's sneakers! Unlike most of the other dinosaurs we're talking about, there have been hundreds of fossils! These are from the **Liaoning fossil beds** in **China**. It lived in the Early Cretaceous period,
between 125- and 120-million years ago.

The microraptor was feathered. Scientists think all feathered dinosaurs were warm blooded, just like birds, and mammals. Because feathers can *sometimes* leave behind traces of color, some of these fossils actually show that some microraptors were black.

A *true* raptor, the microraptor was a carnivore, and it ate the small mammals that were alive in its time. Scientists even found one with the skeleton of an **eomaia** ("dawn mother") in its tummy!

The microraptor had *four* wings! Scientists don't know if it was a flyer or a glider, but they do know it must have been a very clumsy runner. Some insects have four wings, but do you want to know how many other dinosaurs (or birds) have four wings?

Zero. That's how many.

N is for Nuthetes

(new-THEH-tees)

Nn

An early theropod, and quite possibly the earliest raptor, **nuthetes** ("monitor") lived over 140 million years ago (the Early Cretaceous period), in the woodlands of western **Europe.** Fossils were first found in **England** in 1854, later in **France**. These have been primarily fossilized teeth and jaw fragments.

Because of its **serrated** (jagged) teeth, we know it was a carnivore.

Since scientists know it was similar in size to other dinosaurs of its type, they are able to *guess* it was about six-and-a-half feet in length, bipedal, and depending on the skeleton, probably between 30- and 100-pounds in weight.

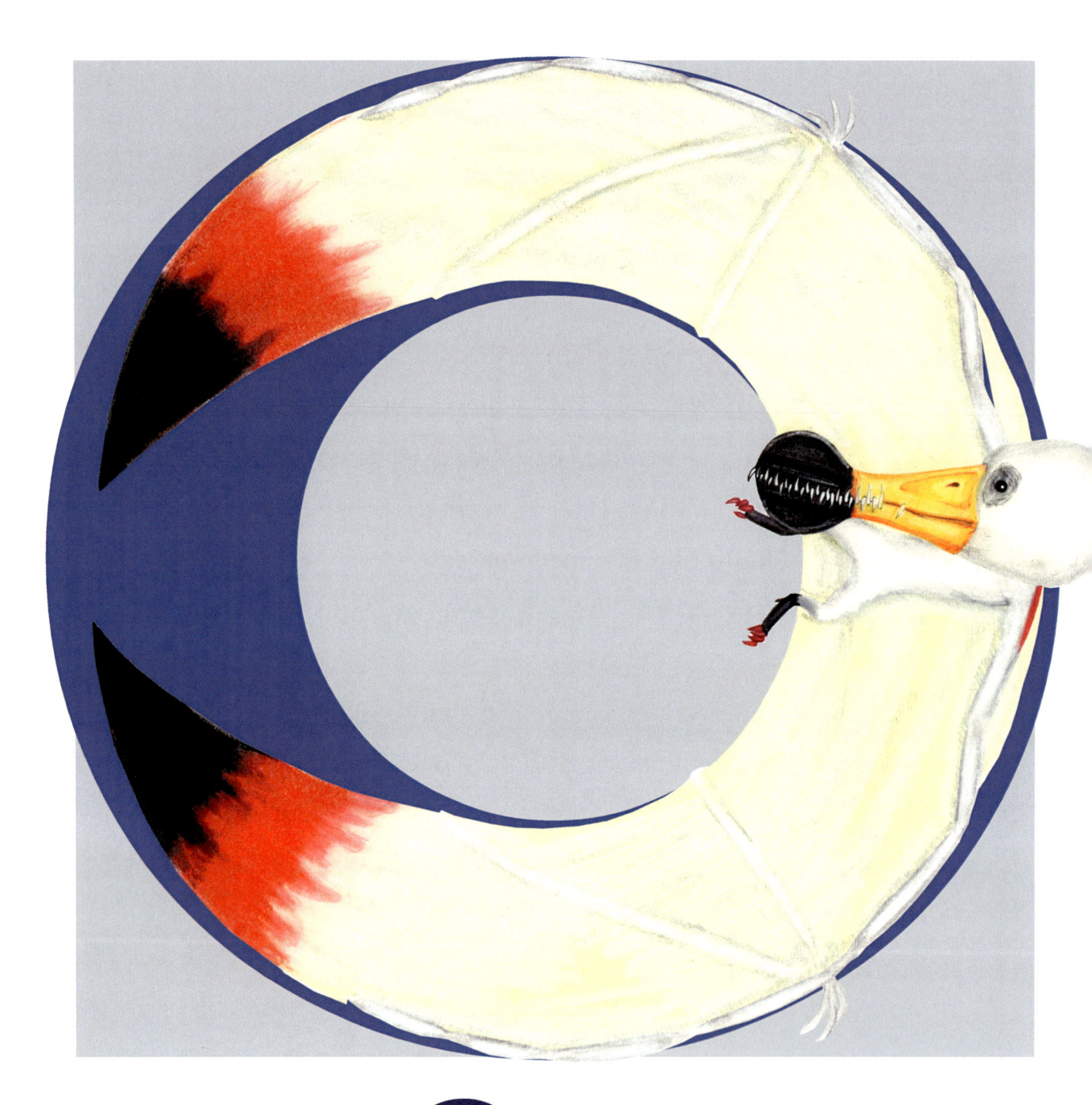

O is for Ornithocheirus
(OR-nith-oh-CARE-us)

Oo

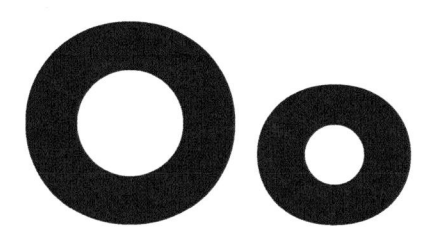

O is for **Ornithocheirus** (OR-nith-oh-CARE-us),
Ojoceratops (OH-ho-SEH-rah-tops),
and **Oohkotokia** (OH-oh-coe-TOE-kee-ah), too!

First discovered in the early 1800s, the **ornithocheirus** ("bird hand") was a **pterosaur** (TARE-oh-saur), a **flying reptile**. It lived along the coasts of the United Kingdom and possibly Morocco. It lived about 120 million years ago, during the Early Cretaceous period.   While not the largest pterosaur ever, the ornithocheirus was the
largest flying reptile of its time. Bigger than any *modern* bird, it had a wingspan of between 10- and 20-feet, and weighed somewhere between 50- and 100-pounds!
It mostly ate fish. Incredibly, it *did* have that funny-looking bump on its nose! It probably used it to crack **shellfish**.

P is for Pachycephalosaurus
(PACK-ee-SEF-fuh-low-SORE-us)

Pp

P is for **Pachycephalosaurus** (PACK-ee-SEFFA-low-SORE-us),
Phuwiangosaurus (FOO-wee-ANG-oh-SORE-us),
and **Pteranodon** (teh-RAN-oh-don), too!

Look at that big head! **Pachycephalosaurus** means "thick-headed lizard," and it is easy to see why. Its skull was 10-inches thick on top (that's *thick*)! They don't really know why it had such a thick skull. Many think pachycephalosaurus probably used it to butt heads, like rams do.

Pachycephalosaurus was a **North-American**, bipedal, herbivore. It probably weighed about two tons. It lived in the Late Cretaceous period, about 100-to-66 million years ago.

Now, scientists have only a skull for this dinosaur. Which isn't much. But you would think that could give them a lot of information about a dinosaur... Right?

Not so much.

Oddly, scientists seem to know more about dinosaurs for which they have *only* bone fragments!

That does *not* make sense!

Q is for Quetzlcoatlus
(KET-sull-co-WAD-dle-us)

Qq

Q is for **Quetzlcoatlus** (KET-sull-co-WAD-dle-us),

and **Qantassaurus** (KWAHN-tuh-SORE-us), too!

The quetzalcoatlus was the. Single. Largest. Flying. Creature. Ever!
The quetzalcoatlus was 16-feet tall, with a wingspan that stretched 36 feet!
The quetzalcoatlus was the size of a small airplane!

The qantassaurus was only about 3-feet tall and 6-feet long.
The qantassasaurus could *not* fly.

The quetzalcoatlus was named after **Quetzalcoatl**, the **serpent god** of ancient **Mexico**. It lived in the Late Cretaceous period, between 73- and 66-million years ago. It was first discovered in Texas.
The qantassaurus was named after the **Australian** airline, Qantas.

Now, if *you* were going to name a dinosaur for an **airline**, why wouldn't you pick a *flying* reptile?

I'm just sayin'.

Qantassaurus (*not* flying)

R is for Rinchenia

(rin-CHEN-nee-ah)

Rr

The **rinchenia** was discovered by **paleontologist** Rinchen Barsbold. He named it after himself as a joke, but the name stuck!

Rinchenia was a **feathered dinosaur,** and measured between five- and six-feet long and weighed between 22- and 100-pounds. Feathered dinosaurs, or "**dino-birds**," were an important link between small theropods and the birds we all know and love today. These include the archaeopteryx, the elmisaurus, and the kol. In a few pages, we'll see the **xiaotingia**.

Scientists believe because the rinchenia's jaw was so big and strong, it was an omnivore, using those jaws to crush nuts, seeds, and even other dinosaurs! It was discovered in modern Mongolia. It lived in the Late Cretaceous period, about 70-million years ago.

S is for Spinosaurus
(SPY-no-SORE-us)

Ss

S is for **Spinosaurus** (SPY-no-SORE-us),
and **Shaochilong** (SH-OW-chee-LONG), too!

    The **spinosaurus** lived during the Late Cretaceous period, between 100- and 94-million years ago. It was the largest theropod to have ever lived. It was also the largest land-carnivore to have ever lived!

It was bigger than the *T-rex* (The largest North-American theropod).
It was bigger than the **Giganotosaurus** ("GEE-gah-NO-toe-SORE-us").
(The largest *South*-American theropod).
It was *a lot* bigger than your dad. (lol)

    It was up to 46-feet long and weighed up to *ten* tons. That's like *ten cars!*

    Spinosaurus may have spent more time in the water than on land. It ate fish, birds, mammals, and possibly even other dinosaurs, too.

    It was first discovered in **Egypt** shortly before World War I, and later in **Morocco.** The first fossils were shipped to **Germany,** but destroyed by **Allied bombers** in 1944. Luckily, they had made **plaster casts** of the fossils first.

    Whew! Talk about a close one!

T is for Tyrannosaurus Rex
(tie-RAN-no-SORE-us-rex)

Tt

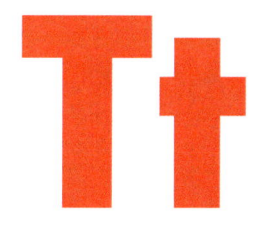

T is for **Tyrannosaurus rex** (tie-RAN-no-SORE-us-rex), and **Thecodontosarus** (Th-ee-co-don-toe-sore-us), too!

The tyrannosaurus rex (or T-Rex, for short) is the most famous dinosaur. Period. (if it were a rock star, it would get the *biggest* dressing room!)

Tyrannosaurus rex ("tyrant lizard king") had jaws so strong, it could crunch through bone! I don't mean little bones, either. I mean the *big* bones of the *five-ton* **quadruped, triceratops**! (try-SARE-uh-tops)

It lived about 80- to 66-million years ago, during the Late Cretaceous period, in the **United States** & **Canada**. It was a carnivore, big enough to eat pretty much any animal it wanted.

One of the largest theropods, It was about 40-feet long, and probably weighed nine tons. **Tyrannosaurs** were the only theropods with only two fingerson each hand. This includes not just T-Rex, but the **albertosaurus** (al-BER-toe-SORE-us), the **gorgosaurus,** (GORE-go-Sore-us), and a bunch of others.

Scientists now think its arms were longer than they used to, but the T-Rex's arms were *still* too short to brush its teeth.

...and just forget about flossing!

U is for Utahceratops
(YOU-taw-SARA-tops)

U u

U is for **Utahceratops** (YOU-taw-SARA-tops), and **Unenlagia** (ooh-nen-LAH-jee-uh), too!

Okay. I was not able to talk about *my second*-favorite dinosaur, the triceratops. Luckily, there were *dozens* of **ceratopsian** ("horn-faced") dinosaurs!

This is the **Utahceratops** ("horned face from Utah"). Strangely enough, the Utahceratops came from **Utah**! It lived there during the Late Cretaceous period, between 76- and 75-million years ago. It stood 6-feet tall at the shoulder, and was between 18- and 22-feet in length. It had a big, plate-looking thing on the back of its skull called a **frill**.

Including that frill, its skull was over seven-feet long. That is *probably* taller than your dad! Like the triceratops ("three-horned face"), it was a quadrupedal herbivore.

Way back in the 20th century, they told us dinosaurs were cold-blooded. *Now* they think the utahceratops, and so many others, was *warm*-blooded.

My life has been one big lie!

V is for Velociraptor
(veh-LOSS-ih-rap-ter)

Vv

Do not let that movie fool you.

Sure, the **velociraptor** ("swift thief") was really cool, but it was *not* six-feet tall. It was *not* clever. (It was *probably* dumber than your neighbor's cat!) It could not use a door knob, even if there were door knobs when it lived, 73-million years ago, during the Late Cretaceous period.

The velociraptors in "Jurassic Park" were actually more like the Deinonychus (die-NON-ih-kuss).

Deinonychus was a much-larger raptor, but still feathered (Did I mention the feathers?). Just like today's birds, the velociraptor had bumps on its bones, where feathers would have attached.

Scientists think the velociraptor was about two-feet tall, six-feet long, including the tail, and weighed around 30 pounds.

The velociraptor was found in Mongolia in 1924. It used those big, curved, hind claws to attack and kill prey like the **Protoceratops**, the **ancestor** of other ceratopsian dinosaurs like the triceratops, and Utahceratops.

W is for Wenupteryx
(we-NUP-ter-ix)

Ww

This is a **wenupteryx** ("fast sky"). Fast sky? Maybe I should have given it racing stripes! It was a small **pterosaur,** a flying reptile, from the coast of southern **Argentina**. It was a **piscitore**, which means it mostly ate fish (yum! Fish!), but small animals and bugs were part of its diet.

Its wingspan was almost four feet. There is not much information on its weight… but paleontologists think it weighed just under four-and-one-half pounds.

The wenupteryx lived about 147-million years ago, during the late Jurassic period.

Other than that, I got nothing!

X is for Xiaotingia

(zhow-TIN-jee-ah)

Xx

The **xiaotingia** (named after paleontologist Zheng Xiaoting) was yet another, small, feathered dinosaur. Following a lot of confusion, scientists now say it was one of the earliest ancestors of modern *birds*. However, the xiaotingia was only *distantly* related to the pterosaurs, or flying reptiles.

The xiaotingia lived in **China**, during the Middle-to-Late Jurassic Period, 155- to 150-million years ago. It was an **insectivorous**, (insect-eating) Yuck! creature about the size of a large modern-day **pigeon**.

Scientists are pretty sure the xiaotingia was predominantly black.

...But this book is *still* in color!

(...Bugs? Well, bugs are *still* icky!)

Y is for Yangchuanosaurus
(YANG-chwan-oh-SORE-us)

Yy

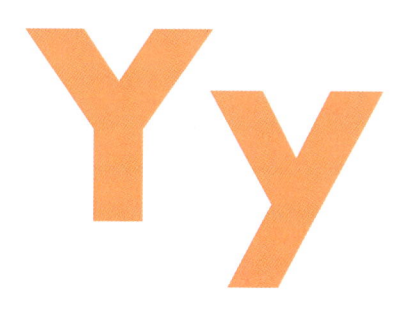

Like the allosaurus in North America, the theropod **Yangchuanosaurus** ("lizard from Yangchuan") was an apex predator that hunted the different sauropods and **stegosaurs** where it lived about 165- 145-million years ago, during the Late Jurassic and early Cretaceous periods.

The allosaurus of Asia, it was found in the **Yangchuan** area of eastern China.

An apex predator, the Yangchuanosaurus was about 30-feet long, and weighed about three tons, with a long, powerful tail.

Unlike other theropods, the Yangchuangosaurus hunted in packs! Can you imagine how scary that was? What if you were chased by not one; not two; but three? Or more?

It's enough to make a stegosaurus want to just stay home, thanks.

Z is for Zarafasaura
(ZARR-ruh-fuh-SORE-uh)

Zz

Elasmosaurs, (eh-LAS-moe-sores) were a large type of extra-long necked **Plesiosaur** (PLEH-see-oh-sore), and the **Zarafasaura** ("giraffe lizard") was a small elasmosaur. Zarafasaura was discovered in Morocco, where there was once a big sea. It lived about 72- to 66-million years ago, during the Late Cretaceous period.

Zarafasaura was one big, ugly, marine reptile. It was about 13-feet long, and weighed about 220 pounds. It was longer than any modern **Alligator**! Its teeth stuck out all over its mouth, and it *really* could have used **braces**... Really *big* braces! Its **flippers** were like a **sea lion's**, and had foot bones in them. (Even toes!)

Sorry, but there is no evidence of toe*nails,* so they could not have been decorated with polish or jewels. Quite frankly, the only color this mean-looking dinosaur would go for is black.

Hey Kids!

For more information, prints, custom "monograminals," downloads, and fun learning activities, please visit Mr. Crowder at **AuthorMikeCrowder.com**

Would you like Mr. Crowder to bring all this **fun** to your school? Share this book with your teachers, and he *just might* be *crazy* enough to visit your school!

Contact Mr. Crowder at

AuthorMikeCrowder.com

About the Author

Although already the darling of smart folks everywhere, it wasn't until his actual birth in 1963 that Mr. Crowder began to meet with any popular acclaim.

He was raised in Florida...

In a barn...

By wolves...

Or apes...

Mr Crowder and His fabulous wife, Gwen, currently live somewhere in the Southeast with his dogs, Bo & Luke.

Made in the USA
Middletown, DE
06 April 2025